The Exciting Brazilian Culinary World

Homemade Brazilian Recipes

BY: SOPHIA FREEMAN

© 2019 Sophia Freeman All Rights Reserved

COPYRIGHTED

Liability

This publication is meant as an informational tool. The individual purchaser accepts all liability if damages occur because of following the directions or guidelines set out in this publication. The Author bears no responsibility for reparations caused by the misuse or misinterpretation of the content.

Copyright

The content of this publication is solely for entertainment purposes and is meant to be purchased by one individual. Permission is not given to any individual who copies, sells or distributes parts or the whole of this publication unless it is explicitly given by the Author in writing.

My gift to you!

Thank you, cherished reader, for purchasing my book and taking the time to read it. As a special reward for your decision, I would like to offer a gift of free and discounted books directly to your inbox. All you need to do is fill in the box below with your email address and name to start getting amazing offers in the comfort of your own home. You will never miss an offer because a reminder will be sent to you. Never miss a deal and get great deals without having to leave the house! Subscribe now and start saving!

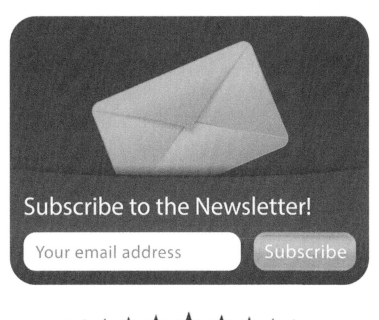

Table of Contents

Delicious Brazilian Food Recipes 6

1) Brazilian Beef Pastitsada 7

2) Brazilian Stroganoff.. 10

3) Brazilian Mashed Potato and Beef Casserole 13

4) Brazilian Pork.. 17

5) Easy Brazilian Chicken 20

6) Brazilian Shrimp Soup 23

7) Brazilian Garlic and Butter Steak 26

8) Brazilian Cheese Bread 29

9) Brazilian Rice, Beans and Sausage................................. 32

10) Brazilian Sweet and Sour Meatballs 35

11) Brazilian Ham and Cheese Rolls 37

12) One Pot Brazilian Sausage with Rice.......................... 41

13) Brazilian Paprika Chicken Stew 44

14) Brazilian Chicken Enchiladas 48

15) Brazilian Saffron Rice with Chicken 52

16) Brazilian Beer Marinated Chicken.............................. 56

17) Brazilian Quindim.. 59

18) Waffle Pao de Queijo 62

19) Brazilian Chicken Coxinhas... 64

20) Brazilian Mac and Cheese 68

21) Brazilian Chocolate Trifle.. 72

22) Brazilian Beef Kibbe 76

23) Brazilian Rabanada 81

24) Brazilian Sopa de Fuba.. 84

25) Brazilian Chocolate Fudge Flan 87

About the Author.. 90

Author's Afterthoughts... 92

Delicious Brazilian Food Recipes

1) Brazilian Beef Pastitsada

To end things off, we have this delicious and hearty beef dish that even the pickiest of eaters will fall in love with. Serve this dish with mashed potatoes or rice for the tastiest results.

Yield: 4 servings

Preparation Time: 35 minutes

Ingredient List:

- 2 Tablespoons of extra virgin olive oil
- 1 ¾ pounds of beef steak
- 12 shallots, peeled
- 2 teaspoons of ground allspice
- 1 cup of red wine
- 1 ¾ pounds of tomatoes, peeled and seeds removed
- ½ pint of beef stock
- 1 tablespoon of white sugar, optional

zzzzzzzzzzzzzzzzzzzzzzzzzzzzzzzzzzzzzzzzzzzzzzzzz

Instructions:

1. Preheat the oven to 300 degrees.

2. Place a large cast iron skillet over medium heat. Add in the olive oil and once hot, add in the beef. Cook for 8 to 10 minutes or until browned. Remove the beef and transfer to a large plate.

3. Add in the peeled shallots. Cook for 2 to 3 minutes or until soft.

4. Add in the cooked beef and stir well to mix.

5. Add in the ground allspice, red wine, tomatoes and beef stock. Deglaze the bottom of the skillet and stir well to incorporate.

6. Transfer into the oven. Bake for 3 ½ hours or until thick in consistency. Season with the white sugar if you wish.

7. Remove and serve immediately.

2) Brazilian Stroganoff

Unlike its German counterpart, this stroganoff dish is packed full of a Brazilian flavor that is impossible to resist. Feel free to leave out the mushrooms if you wish.

Yield: 5 servings

Preparation Time: 30 minutes

Ingredient List:

- 2.2 pounds of lean sirloin, cut into thin strips
- Dash of salt and black pepper
- 2 Tablespoons of vegetable oil
- 2 cloves of garlic, minced
- 1 white onion, chopped
- 2 ½ cups of sour cream
- 1/3 cup of ketchup
- 3 Tablespoons of mustard
- 2 teaspoons of Worcestershire sauce
- 2 cups of mushrooms, thinly sliced

zzzzzzzzzzzzzzzzzzzzzzzzzzzzzzzzzzzzzzzzzzzzzzzz

Instructions:

1. Season the sirloin strips with a dash of salt and black pepper.

2. Place a large skillet over medium heat. Add in a tablespoon of the vegetable oil. Once hot, add in the season sirloin strips. Cook for 8 to 10 minutes or until browned. Remove and transfer to a plate.

3. Using the same skillet, add in the remaining oil. Add the garlic in and cook for 1 to 2 minutes or until browned.

4. Add in the onions and then cook for 5 to 10 minutes or until transparent.

5. Add in the browned meat, the sour cream, ketchup, mustard and Worcestershire sauce. Stir well to mix. Add in the mushrooms and stir again until incorporated. Continue to cook for 5 minutes or until the mushrooms are soft.

6. Remove from heat and serve immediately.

3) Brazilian Mashed Potato and Beef Casserole

This is a delicious casserole dish you can make whenever you need to feed a large group of people. Packed full of hearty beef and mashed potatoes, this is one dish the entire family will be begging for.

Yield: 6 servings

Preparation Time: 1 hour

Ingredients for the meat:

- 1 ½ pounds of lean ground beef
- 1 cups of tomatoes, chopped
- 1 onion, chopped
- 3 cloves of garlic, minced
- 2 tomatoes, chopped
- 1 ½ Tablespoons of all-purpose flour
- 2 Tablespoons of butter
- 1/3 cup of parsley, chopped
- 1 sprig of rosemary, minced
- 1 ½ cup of Parmesan cheese, grated
- 1 egg yolk, large
- Dash of salt and black pepper

Ingredients for the mashed potatoes:

- 1 ½ pounds of russet potatoes
- 1, 8-ounce pack of cream cheese
- 1 cup of heavy cream
- Dash of nutmeg
- Dash of salt and black pepper
- 2 cups of mozzarella cheese, shredded

zzzzzzzzzzzzzzzzzzzzzzzzzzzzzzzzzzzzzzzzzzzzzzzzz

Instructions:

1. Preheat the oven to 375 degrees.

2. Place a large pot over medium to high heat. Fill with salted water. Bring the water to a boil and add in the potatoes. Cook for 20 minutes or until softened. Remove the potatoes and peel them. Transfer to a large bowl and mash until smooth in consistency.

3. Place a large saucepan over medium heat. Add in the heavy cream and cream cheese. Stir to mix and cook for 3 minutes or until the cream cheese dissolves.

4. Add the cream cheese mixture to the mashed potatoes. Stir well until smooth in consistency. Season with a dash of salt and black pepper.

5. Place a large skillet over medium heat. Add in the butter and once melted, add in the onion and garlic. Stir to mix and cook for 5 minutes or until translucent.

6. Add in the tomatoes, chopped parsley and minced rosemary. Stir to mix and cook for 2 minutes.

7. Add in the lean ground beef. Cook for 8 to 10 minutes or until browned.

8. Add in the all-purpose flour, grated Parmesan cheese and crushed tomatoes. Stir well until fully incorporated. Continue to cook for 5 minutes or until thick in consistency. Add in the large egg yolk. Season with a dash of salt and black pepper.

9. Transfer the mixture into a large cast iron skillet. Top off with the mashed potatoes and the shredded mozzarella cheese.

10. Place into the oven to bake for 30 minutes or until the cheese is melted. Remove and serve right away.

4) Brazilian Pork

To kick things off we have a delicious and mouthwatering Brazilian braised pork dish that will leave you craving for more. Made with passion fruit and guajillo chiles, this dish is to die for!

Yield: 8 servings

Preparation Time: 4 hours and 10 minutes

Ingredient List:

- 4-pound pork shoulder
- 1 tablespoon of extra virgin olive oil
- 1 tablespoon of salt
- 1 tablespoon of dried oregano
- 1 teaspoon of ground cumin
- 1, 11.5 ounce can of Passion fruit and Orange juice cocktail concentrate
- 8 guajillo chiles, soaked
- 10 cloves of garlic
- 1 jalapeño pepper, stems removed
- 2 onions, chopped

zzzzzzzzzzzzzzzzzzzzzzzzzzzzzzzzzzzzzzzzzzzzzzzzz

Instructions:

1. Add the guajillos into a large bowl. Cover with hot water and set aside to soak for 30 minutes. Remove and transfer into a food processor.

2. Add in the cloves of garlic, jalapeño pepper, can of orange concentrate and ½ cup of water. Blender on the highest setting until smooth in consistency. Set this mixture aside.

3. Preheat the oven to 325 degrees.

4. Slice the pork into 8 pieces and place into a large roasting pan. Season with dash of salt, dried oregano and ground cumin. Pour the chili sauce over the top and top off with the sliced onions.

5. Place into the oven to roast for 4 hours.

6. Remove and serve immediately.

5) Easy Brazilian Chicken

This is a simple dish that you can make whenever you are craving authentic Brazilian food. It has a hint of orange tang that is impossible to resist.

Yield: 4 servings

Preparation Time: 2 hours and 20 minutes

Ingredient List:

- 1 lemon, fresh and zest
- 1 lime, fresh and zest
- 1, 8 ounce can of tomato sauce
- 1, 6 ounce can of orange juice concentrate
- 1 ½ cloves of garlic, minced
- 1 teaspoon of dried Italian seasoning
- 1 teaspoon of hot sauce
- 4 chicken breasts, boneless and skinless
- ¾ cup of chunky salsa

zzzzzzzzzzzzzzzzzzzzzzzzzzzzzzzzzzzzzzzzzzzzzzzzz

Instructions:

1. Add the fresh lime and lemon zest into a large Ziploc bag.

2. Squeeze the fresh lime juice and lemon juice into the Ziploc bag.

3. Add in the remaining ingredients except for the chicken and salsa. Stir well to mix.

4. Add in the chicken and seal the bag. Set into the fridge to marinate for 2 hours.

5. Preheat and outdoor grill to medium or high heat.

6. Place the marinated chicken onto the grill. Cook for 10 to 15 minutes or until cooked through. Baste the chicken as it cooks.

7. Remove from the grill and serve with the chunky salsa.

6) Brazilian Shrimp Soup

This is the perfect dish to make whenever you are craving authentic seafood. It is creamy in consistency and packed full of plenty of shrimp and coconut milk.

Yield: 6 servings

Preparation Time: 40 minutes

Ingredient List:

- 2 Tablespoons of extra virgin olive oil
- 1 onion, chopped
- 1 red bell pepper, chopped
- 4 cloves of garlic, minced
- ½ cup of long grain white rice
- ¼ teaspoons of red pepper flakes
- 2 teaspoons of salt
- 1, 15 ounce can of tomatoes, crushed
- 4 cups of water
- 1 cup of unsweetened coconut milk
- 1 pound of shrimp, shells removed and cut into small pieces
- ¼ teaspoons of black pepper
- 1 lemon, juiced
- ½ cup of parsley, chopped and for garnish

zzzzzzzzzzzzzzzzzzzzzzzzzzzzzzzzzzzzzzzzzzzzzzzzz

Instructions:

1. Place a large soup pot over low heat. Add in the olive oil and once hot, add in the chopped onion, chopped red bell pepper and minced garlic. Cook for 5 to 10 minutes or until soft.

2. Add in the white rice, crushed red pepper flakes, dash of salt, can of crushed tomatoes and water. Stir well to mix and bring this mixture to a boil.

3. Cook for 10 minutes or until the rice is cooked through.

4. Add in the coconut milk. Bring the soup back into a simmer. Add in the shrimp.

5. Simmer for 3 to 5 minutes or until the shrimp is bright pink.

6. Add in the fresh lemon juice, chopped parsley and a dash of black pepper.

7. Remove from heat and serve immediately.

7) Brazilian Garlic and Butter Steak

If you are a huge fan of steak, then this is one dish I know you won't be able to get enough of. This recipe makes the juiciest and most delicate steak that you will ever taste.

Yield: 4 servings

Preparation Time: 15 minutes

Ingredient List:

- 6 cloves of garlic, minced
- Dash of salt
- 1 ½ pound of skirt steak, trimmed and cut into small pieces
- Dash of black pepper
- 2 Tablespoons of canola oil
- 4 Tablespoons of unsalted butter
- 1 tablespoon of flat leaf parsley, chopped

zzzzzzzzzzzzzzzzzzzzzzzzzzzzzzzzzzzzzzzzzzzzzzzzz

Instructions:

1. Season the steak with a dash of salt and black pepper.

2. Place a large skillet over medium to high heat. Add in the canola oil and once hot add in the steak. Cook for 2 to 3 minutes on each side or until browned evenly. Remove and transfer the steak to a large plate. Set aside.

3. In the same skillet, add in the butter. Once melted add in the garlic. Cook for 4 minutes or until golden brown. Season with a dash of salt.

4. Slice the steak and serve with a spoonful of the garlic and butter mixture over the top. Garnish with the chopped parsley.

8) Brazilian Cheese Bread

This delicious cheesy bread can be prepared to accompany any other Brazilian dish that you may make. It is gluten free, so it is perfect for those who are on a strict diet.

Yield: 12 servings

Preparation Time: 40 minutes

Ingredient List:

- 1 cup of whole milk
- ½ cup of vegetable oil
- 1 ¼ teaspoons of salt
- 2 cups of tapioca flour
- 1 cup of mozzarella cheese, shredded
- ½ cup of cotija
- 2 eggs, large

zzzzzzzzzzzzzzzzzzzzzzzzzzzzzzzzzzzzzzzzzzzzzzz

Instructions:

1. Preheat the oven to 350 degrees. Line a large baking sheet with a sheet of parchment paper. Set aside.

2. Place a large saucepan over medium to high heat. Add in the whole milk, vegetable oil and dash of salt. Stir well to mix.

3. Quickly add in the tapioca flour and stir well until a dough begins to form.

4. Transfer the dough to the bowl of a stand mixer. Beat with a dough hook for 2 to 3 minutes or until the dough is smooth. Add in the shredded mozzarella and beat to incorporate.

5. Add in the eggs and continue to beat for another 2 to 3 minutes.

6. Divide the dough into small pieces. Place the balls onto the baking sheet.

7. Place into the oven to bake for 25 to 30 minutes or until golden.

8. Remove from the oven and set aside to cool before serving.

9) Brazilian Rice, Beans and Sausage

This is a simple and easy dish to prepare, especially if you are constantly on the go. It is so easy to make, it can be prepared in just under 30 minutes.

Yield: 4 servings

Preparation Time: 30 minutes

Ingredient List:

- 2 Tablespoons of extra virgin olive oil
- 1 pound of smoked sausage, thinly sliced
- ½ cup of green onion, chopped
- 3 cloves of garlic, minced
- 1 cup of white rice
- 2 cups of chicken broth
- 1, 14 ounce can of pinto beans, drained and rinsed
- Dash of salt and black pepper
- 1 to 2 bay leaves

zzzzzzzzzzzzzzzzzzzzzzzzzzzzzzzzzzzzzzzzzzzzzzzzz

Instructions:

1. Place a large skillet over medium heat. Add in the extra virgin olive oil. Once hot, add in the sliced sausage, chopped green onion and minced garlic. Stir well to mix and cook for 10 to 12 minutes or until the sausage is cooked through.

2. Add in the white rice, chicken broth, can of pinto beans and bay leaves. Season with a dash of salt and black pepper. Stir well to mix.

3. Bring the mixture to a boil. Lower the heat to low and then cover. Simmer for 20 to 25 minutes or until the rice is cooked through.

4. Remove from heat and fluff the rice with a fork.

5. Serve immediately.

10) Brazilian Sweet and Sour Meatballs

This is one dish I know you will love to serve during your next family barbecue. Made with a combination of fresh pepper and smothered in a sweet and sour sauce, this is one dish the entire family won't be able to get enough of.

Yield: 4 servings

Preparation Time: 25 minutes

Ingredient List:

- 1 pound of meatballs, cooked
- 1 red bell peppers, cut into small pieces
- 1 green bell pepper, cut into small pieces
- ¼ cup of apricot jam
- ¼ cup of barbecue sauce

Instructions:

1. Preheat an outdoor grill to medium or high heat.

2. Thread the cooked meatballs onto skewers.

3. In a small bowl, add in the apricot jam and barbecue sauce. Stir well to mix and brush the meatballs with the sauce.

4. Place onto the grill and cook for 8 to 10 minutes, making sure to baste with the sauce frequently.

5. Remove and serve immediately.

11) Brazilian Ham and Cheese Rolls

These rolls make for the perfect breakfast whenever you need a convenient dish to take with you as you head out the door. Packed full of ham and melted cheese, everyone who tries this will fall in love with it.

Yield: 20 servings

Preparation Time: 1 hours and 45 minutes

Ingredient List:

- 1, 1.4-ounce pack of active dry yeast
- 2 teaspoons of white sugar
- 1 cup of warm water
- 1 teaspoon of salt
- ¼ cup of vegetable oil
- 3 cups of all-purpose flour
- 10 slices of ham, sliced thinly
- 10 slices of Havarti, shredded
- Dash of dried oregano
- 1 egg + 1 tablespoon of water, mixed together

zzzzzzzzzzzzzzzzzzzzzzzzzzzzzzzzzzzzzzzzzzzzzzzz

Instructions:

1. In the large bowl of a stand mixer, add in the yeast, white sugar and warm water. Stir well to mix and cover. Allow to rest for 10 minutes.

2. Add in the vegetable oil and dash of salt. Stir well to mix.

3. Add in the all-purpose flour and beat on the lowest setting with a dough hook attached. Knead for 6 to 8 minutes or until an elastic dough begins to form.

4. Brush the dough lightly with oil. Cover and set aside to rise for 1 hour.

5. Preheat the oven to 350 degrees. Grease two large baking sheets with cooking spray.

6. Divide the dough into two parts.

7. Roll each piece of dough into a 12-inch rectangle. Cut each rectangle into 10 triangles. Place a slice of ham and a piece of cheese into each triangle. Roll each triangle starting from the widest part. Place onto the greased baking sheets.

8. In a small bowl, add in the egg and remaining water. Whisk until mixed. Brush the rolls with the egg wash mixture. Sprinkle the oregano evenly over the rolls.

9. Place into the oven to bake for 20 minutes or until golden brown.

10. Remove and set aside to cool for 5 minutes before serving.

12) One Pot Brazilian Sausage with Rice

This is the perfect meal to make whenever you need something convenient to make after a hard day at work. It is so delicious; the entire family will fall in love with it.

Yield: 6 servings

Preparation Time: 35 minutes

Ingredient List:

- 1 tablespoon of extra virgin olive oil
- 1 onion, peeled and chopped
- 1 tablespoon of garlic, mashed
- 4 Brazilian sausage, sliced thinly
- 2 cups of bacon, cooked
- 4 cups of long grain white rice
- 2, 32-ounce containers of chicken stock
- Dash of salt
- 2, 8-ounce cans of black beans, drained
- 1 tablespoon of dried oregano
- Green onions, thinly slices and for garnish
- Cilantro, chopped and for garnish
- 2 limes, juice

zzzzzzzzzzzzzzzzzzzzzzzzzzzzzzzzzzzzzzzzzzzzzzzz

Instructions:

1. Place a large skillet over medium to high heat. Add in the olive oil and once hot, add in the onions. Cook for 10 to 15 minutes or until caramelized.

2. Add in the sliced sausage. Cook for 8 to 10 minutes or until browned.

3. Add in the garlic and cook for an additional minute.

4. Add in the white rice and stir well to mix.

5. Add in the canned black beans, dried oregano and chicken stock. Stir well to incorporate. Reduce the heat to low and cover. Cook for 15 to 20 minutes or until the rice is cooked through.

6. Add in the cooked bacon, sliced green onions and chopped cilantro. Squeeze the lime juice over the top and serve immediately.

13) Brazilian Paprika Chicken Stew

This is a perfect stew dish to make whenever you need to be warmed up on a chilly winter night. It is a hearty dish that can be made using only one pot.

Yield: 6 to 8 servings

Preparation Time: 55 minutes

Ingredient List:

- 1 pound of chicken breasts, boneless, skinless and cut into small pieces
- 1 pound of chicken thighs, boneless, skinless and cut into small pieces
- ½ pound of chicken sausage, thinly sliced
- 1 lime, juiced
- Dash of salt and black pepper
- 1/3 cup of vegetable oil
- 1 onion, chopped
- 3 cloves of garlic, minced
- 1 tablespoon of smoked paprika
- 1 tablespoon of tomato paste
- 5 cups of chicken broth
- 2 bay leaves
- 1 tablespoon of thyme leaves
- 1 ½ cups of white beans, cooked
- 1 tablespoon of all-purpose flour
- ¼ cup of parsley, chopped

Instructions:

1. In a large bowl, add in the chicken and sausage pieces. Pour in the fresh lime juice and season with a dash of salt and black pepper. Stir well to mix.

2. Place a large Dutch oven over medium to high heat. Add in the oil and once hot add in the chicken mixture. Cook for 2 to 3 minutes on each side. Remove and transfer to a large plate.

3. Reduce the heat to low. Add in the remaining oil. Followed by the chopped onion and minced garlic. Cook for 3 to 5 minutes or until soft. Add in the smoked paprika and tomato paste. Stir well to mix.

4. Pour in the chicken broth, bay leaves and thyme. Stir to mix and bring to a boil. Reduce the heat to low. Simmer for 30 to 40 minutes or until the chicken is cooked through.

5. Remove one cup of the broth. Add in the flour to this broth and whisk to mix. Return back into the Dutch oven. Add in the cooked white beans. Cook for a further 10 minutes or until thick in consistency.

6. Remove the bay leaves. Season with a dash of salt and black pepper. Add in the chopped parsley.

7. Remove from heat and serve immediately.

14) Brazilian Chicken Enchiladas

This is an excellent mixture of Brazilian and Mexican flavors. It is perfect to make during any night of the week, after a stressful day at the office.

Yield: 4 servings

Preparation Time: 35 minutes

Ingredients for the discs:

- 2 cups of all-purpose flour
- 2 eggs, large
- 2 cups of warm milk
- ¼ teaspoons of salt
- 2 Tablespoons of melted butter

Ingredients for the filling:

- 2 tablespoons of vegetable oil
- 1 pound of chicken breasts, boneless and skinless
- Dash of salt and black pepper
- 2 teaspoons of powdered cumin
- 2 teaspoons of powdered garlic
- 2 teaspoons of powdered onion
- 1 teaspoon of chicken bouillon
- 1 yellow onion, chopped
- 2 cloves of garlic, minced
- 1 cup of frozen corn, thawed
- ¼ cup of green olives, chopped
- ¾ cup of stewed tomatoes, canned
- 1 ½ cups of tomato sauce
- 2 Tablespoons of heavy cream

- 1 cup of mozzarella cheese, shredded
- Parsley, chopped and for garnish

zzzzzzzzzzzzzzzzzzzzzzzzzzzzzzzzzzzzzzzzzzzzzzzz

Instructions:

1. Add all of the ingredients for the discs into a blender. Blend on the highest setting until smooth in consistency.

2. Place a small skillet over medium to high heat. Add in the vegetable oil and once hot, add ¼ cup of the disc mixture into it. Tilt the pan to swirl the mixture around. Cook for 1 to 2 minutes or until brown. Remove from the skillet and set aside. Repeat with the remaining mixture until all of the discs have been made.

3. Season the chicken with a dash of salt and black pepper. Rub the ground cumin, chicken bouillon, minced garlic and powdered onion over the chicken.

4. Place a large skillet over medium heat. Add in the vegetable oil and once hot, add in the chicken. Cook for 8 to 10 minutes or until browned. Remove and transfer to a plate to cool.

5. Add the onion and garlic into the chicken drippings. Cook for 5 minutes or until soft. Add in the thawed corn and chopped olives. Stir well to mix. Add in the tomatoes and cook for an additional minute.

6. Shred the chicken finely using two forks. Add the chicken into the skillet and stir well to incorporate.

7. In a large bowl, add in the tomato sauce and heavy cream. Stir well until mixed.

8. Coat a large baking pan with the tomato sauce.

9. Add ¼ cup of the chicken mixture onto each disc. Roll burrito style and place into the baking dish. Repeat with the remaining chicken and discs. Pour the remaining tomato sauce over the top. Sprinkle the shredded mozzarella cheese and chopped parsley.

10. Place into the oven to bake for 10 minutes at 350 degrees or until the cheese is melted.

11. Remove and serve immediately.

15) Brazilian Saffron Rice with Chicken

This is a traditional dish that is often served in many Brazilian household. Packed full of hearty vegetables, this is a dish you won't have to feel guilty about enjoying.

Yield: 4 to 6 servings

Preparation Time: 1 hour and 5 minutes

Ingredient List:

- 2 pounds of chicken thighs, boneless and skinless
- 1 teaspoon of salt
- Dash of black pepper
- 1 teaspoon of powdered garlic
- ½ teaspoons of ground cumin
- 2 to 3 Tablespoons of vegetable oil
- 1 white onion, chopped
- 1 green bell pepper, chopped
- 2 cloves of garlic, minced
- 2 cups of parboiled rice
- ½ cup of white wine
- 3 ½ cups of chicken broth
- ½ cup of hot water
- 1 tablespoon of tomato paste
- 1 bay leaf
- ½ of a lemon
- 3 tomatoes, peeled and seeds removed
- 1 to 1 ¼ cups of frozen peas, cooked
- ¼ cup of green onions, chopped

zzzzzzzzzzzzzzzzzzzzzzzzzzzzzzzzzzzzzzzzzzzzzzzzz

Instructions:

1. Season the chicken thighs with a dash of salt, black pepper, powdered garlic and ground cumin. Set aside to rest for 30 minutes.

2. Place a large pan over medium to high heat. Add in the chopped onion and chopped green bell pepper. Cook for 3 to 5 minutes or until soft.

3. Add in the chicken and cook for 8 to 10 minutes or until browned. Add in the minced garlic and cook for an additional minute.

4. Add in the rice and cook for 5 minutes or until browned.

5. Pour in the white wine. Cook for 3 to 5 minutes or until the wine evaporates.

6. Pour in the chicken broth and stir well to incorporate.

7. In a small bowl and add in the saffron and warm water. Stir until the saffron dissolves. Pour into the pan along with the tomato paste and bay leaf. Stir well to mix.

8. Bring the mixture to a boil. Reduce the heat to low and cover. Simmer for 15 to 20 minutes or until the rice is cooked through.

9. Remove from heat. Add in the fresh lemon juice, chopped tomato, peas and chopped green onions. Stir well to mix. Serve immediately.

16) Brazilian Beer Marinated Chicken

Whenever you want to impress your significant other with your cooking skills, this is the perfect dish to prepare. Made with a marinade that is packed full of flavor, this meaty recipe will have you wanting to make it as often as possible.

Yield: 4 servings

Preparation Time: 30 minutes

Ingredient List:

- 4 cloves of garlic, smashed
- 4, ¼ inch pieces of ginger, smashed
- 1 onion, thinly sliced
- 1 tablespoon of sweet paprika
- 1 teaspoon of salt
- 1 teaspoon of black pepper
- ½ teaspoons of caraway seeds
- ½ of a green bell pepper, sliced thinly
- ¼ cup of Dijon mustard
- 2 cups of dark lager
- ¼ cup of vegetable oil
- 4, 6-ounce chicken breasts, boneless and skinless
- 2 Tablespoons of unsalted butter, melted
- ¼ cup of cilantro, chopped
- Lime wedges, for serving

zzzzzzzzzzzzzzzzzzzzzzzzzzzzzzzzzzzzzzzzzzzzzzzzzz

Instructions:

1. In a large shallow dish, add in the smashed garlic, smashed ginger, sliced onion, sweet paprika, dash of salt, dash of black pepper, caraway seeds, sliced green bell pepper, Dijon mustard, lager and vegetable oil. Whisk well until mixed.

2. Add the chicken into the marinade and cover. Set into the fridge to marinate for 4 hours.

3. Preheat an outdoor grill to medium or high heat.

4. Place the marinated chicken onto the grill. Grill for 5 minutes on each side or until golden brown.

5. Transfer the cooked chicken to a plate. Brush the melted butter over the top.

6. Serve with a garnish of cilantro and the lime wedges.

17) Brazilian Quindim

There is no other traditional Brazilian dish that is quite like this. It is a delicious pastry that is perfect for satisfying your sweet tooth.

Yield: 6 to 8 servings

Preparation Time: 1 hour and 30 minutes

Ingredient List:

- 8 egg yolks, sieved
- 3/5 cup of white sugar
- 3 Tablespoons of melted butter
- ½ cup of coconut milk
- 1 cup of coconut, shredded

Ingredients for the molds:

- 2 Tablespoons of soft butter
- ½ cup of white sugar

zzzzzzzzzzzzzzzzzzzzzzzzzzzzzzzzzzzzzzzzzzzzzzzzz

Instructions:

1. In a large bowl, add in the coconut milk and shredded coconut. Stir well to mix. Set aside to stand for 5 minutes.

2. In a large blender, add in the white sugar, egg yolks, melted butter and coconut mixture. Blend on the highest setting until smooth in consistency.

3. Preheat the oven to 350 degrees.

4. Grease each mold with butter. Rub the edges and the bottom with the remaining white sugar.

5. Pour the coconut mixture into the molds. Set aside to rise for 10 minutes.

6. Pour boiling water into a large roasting pan. Gently add the molds into the water, making sure the water doesn't flow into the molds. Allow to sit for 50 minutes.

7. Remove and set aside to cool before serving.

18) Waffle Pao de Queijo

These delicious Brazilian style waffles are perfect to make nearly every morning. Serve these waffles with your favorite maple syrup for the tastiest results.

Yield: 6 to 8 servings

Preparation Time: 10 minutes

Ingredient List:

- ½ cup of whole milk
- ¼ cup of vegetable oil
- 2 eggs, large
- 1 cup of tapioca flour
- 1 cup of Parmesan cheese, shredded
- ½ teaspoons of salt

zzzzzzzzzzzzzzzzzzzzzzzzzzzzzzzzzzzzzzzzzzzzzzzzz

Instructions:

1. Add all of the ingredients into a blender. Blend on the highest setting until smooth in consistency.

2. Grease a waffle iron with cooking spray and heat to medium or high heat.

3. Pour ½ cup of the batter onto the iron. Close and cook for 4 to 5 minutes or until the waffles are golden brown.

4. Repeat with the remaining waffle batter.

5. Serve the waffles with your favorite maple syrup.

19) Brazilian Chicken Coxinhas

This delicious dish is often sold by street vendors in Brazil. Made with a drumstick wrapped in a savory dough, this is a dish everyone will love.

Yield: 24 servings

Preparation Time: 2 hours

Ingredient List:

- 1 ½ pounds of chicken breasts, cut into halves
- 4 to 5 cups of chicken broth
- 1 carrot, chopped
- 2 onions, chopped
- 2 bay leaves
- 2 Tablespoons of butter
- 2 cloves of garlic, minced
- 1 lime, juiced
- 1, 8-ounce pack of cream cheese, soft
- 2 to 3 cups of all-purpose
- 2 eggs, large
- 2 to 3 cups of grated bread crumbs
- Vegetable oil, for frying
- Dash of salt and black pepper

ZZZZZZZZZZZZZZZZZZZZZZZZZZZZZZZZZZZZZZZZZZZZZZZ

Instructions:

1. Place a shallow pot over medium heat. Add in the chicken breasts. Pour the chicken broth over the top. Add in the carrots, onions and bay leaves. Stir well to mix.

2. Bring the mixture to a simmer for 15 to 20 minutes or until the chicken is cooked through. Remove the chicken and set aside. Strain the broth into a large bowl. Discard the solids.

3. Shred the chicken finely with two forks. Transfer into a large bowl. Add in the soft cream cheese and fresh lime juice. Stir well to mix.

4. Place a large skillet over medium heat. Add in two tablespoons of butter. Once melted add in the chopped onion and minced garlic. Cook for 5 minutes or until soft and translucent. Transfer to the chicken mixture and stir well to mix.

5. Place a large saucepan over medium heat. Add in the chicken broth mixture and bring to a boil. Add in the flour and whisk until smooth in consistency. Cook for 3 minutes or until a dough begins to form. Remove from heat and place the dough into the fridge to chill for 1 hour.

6. Take a small piece of the dough and roll into a ball. Hollow out the center and add 1 ½ teaspoons of the filling right into the center. Roll the dough around the ball. Repeat with the remaining dough and filling.

7. In a small bowl, add in the eggs. Whisk to beat. In a small bowl, add in the breadcrumbs. Season with a dash of salt and black pepper.

8. Dip the coxinhas in the eggs and roll in the breadcrumbs, coating evenly on all sides.

9. Place a large pot over medium to high heat. Fill with vegetable oil and heat until it reaches 350 degrees. Add in the coxinhas and fry for 5 minutes or until golden brown.

10. Remove and transfer to a large plate lined with paper towels to drain. Serve immediately.

20) Brazilian Mac and Cheese

If you love the taste of mac and cheese, then this is one recipe I know you and your family will love. Smothered in plenty of gooey cheese, this is a dish that will surely please even the pickiest of eaters.

Yield: 6 servings

Preparation Time: 35 minutes

Ingredient List:

- 1, 16-ounce box of penne pasta
- 1 tablespoon of extra virgin olive oil
- 2 cloves of garlic, minced
- ¼ cup of red wine
- 1 ½ cup of tomato sauce
- Dash of salt and black pepper
- ¼ cup of basil, chopped
- ½ cup of heavy cream
- 1, 8.5-ounce pack of cheese spread
- 8 ounces of mozzarella cheese, shredded
- 8 ounces of rotisserie chicken, shredded
- 1/3 cup of Parmesan cheese, shredded

zzzzzzzzzzzzzzzzzzzzzzzzzzzzzzzzzzzzzzzzzzzzzzz

Instructions:

1. Preheat the oven to 350 degrees.

2. Cook the penne pasta according to the directions on the package.

3. Place a medium saucepan over medium to high heat. Add in the olive oil. Once hot add in the garlic and cook for 30 seconds.

4. Pour in the red wine and cook for 1 minute or until evaporated. Add in the tomato sauce, chopped basil and a dash of salt and black pepper. Stir to mix and bring this mixture to a boil. Reduce the heat to low and cover. Cook for 5 minutes at a simmer.

5. Add in the heavy cream, cheese spread and shredded mozzarella cheese. Stir well until smooth in consistency. Add in the chicken and toss to mix.

6. Add the pasta into a large baking dish. Pour the cheese sauce over the top and toss to coat. Sprinkle the shredded Parmesan cheese over the top.

7. Cover with a sheet of aluminum foil and place into the oven to bake for 20 minutes. Remove the foil and continue to bake for 5 minutes.

8. Remove from the oven and serve immediately.

21) Brazilian Chocolate Trifle

This is a delicious dessert dish that you can make whenever you are craving something sweet. It resembles a classic tiramisu but is packed with a delicious Brazilian flavor that I know you will fall in love with.

Yield: 8 servings

Preparation Time: 2 hours and 10 minutes

Ingredients for the chocolate layer:

- 20 ladyfinger biscuits
- 2 to 2 Tablespoons of cognac
- 2 cups of whole milk
- 1 ½ cups of powdered cocoa

Ingredients for the cream layer:

- 2, 6-ounce cans of sweet condensed milk
- 4 cups of whole milk
- 2 Tablespoons of cornstarch
- 4 egg yolks, strained

Ingredients for the whipped cream layer:

- 1, 6-ounce container of heavy cream
- 1 cup of powdered sugar
- ½ teaspoons of pure vanilla

ZZZZZZZZZZZZZZZZZZZZZZZZZZZZZZZZZZZZZZZZZZZZZZZZZZ

Instructions:

1. Place a large pot over medium heat. Add in the condensed milk and three cups of whole milk. Stir well to mix.

2. In a small bowl, add in the cornstarch and 1 cup of whole milk. Stir well until the cornstarch dissolves. Pour into the large pot. Cook for 5 minutes or until thick in consistency.

3. Remove one cup of the mixture and set aside to cool. Add in the egg yolks to the cooled mixture and stir well to mix. Return back to the large pot. Continue to cook for another 2 to 3 minutes or until thick in consistency.

4. Remove from heat and set aside to cool. Pour into a large baking dish.

5. In a large bowl, add the biscuits and then add the cognac into a separate large bowl.

6. In the same large pot, add in two cups of whole milk and the powdered cocoa. Stir well to mix.

7. Dip the biscuits into the chocolate mixture and place on top of the cream in the baking dish.

8. Cover and place into the fridge to chill overnight.

9. In a large bowl, add in the heavy cream, powdered sugar and pure vanilla. Beat with an electric mixer on the highest setting until fluffy in consistency. Pour over the biscuits in the baking dish.

10. Cover and place into the fridge to chill for 1 hour before serving.

22) Brazilian Beef Kibbe

This is a dish incorporates three different classic cuisines: Portuguese, African and native Indian. It is a delicious appetizer that you can make any day of the week.

Yield: 45 servings

Preparation Time: 1 hour and 50 minutes

Ingredients for the sauce:

- ½ cup of plain Greek yogurt
- ½ cup of sour cream
- 1 tablespoon of Dijon mustard
- 1 tablespoon of red onion, chopped
- 2 Tablespoons of mint leaves, chopped
- A few drops of lemon juice
- A few drops of hot sauce
- Dash of salt and black pepper

Ingredients for the Kibbe:

- 1 cup of ground bulgur
- 1 pound of lean ground beef
- ½ of a yellow onion, chopped
- 1 scallion, green and white parts separated and chopped
- 2 cloves of garlic, minced
- 1 teaspoon of dried oregano
- ¼ cup of mint leaves, chopped
- ¼ cup of extra virgin olive oil
- 2 teaspoons of salt
- Dash of black pepper
- Dash of cayenne pepper
- A few drops of hot sauce
- 2 cups of canola oil, for frying

zzzzzzzzzzzzzzzzzzzzzzzzzzzzzzzzzzzzzzzzzzzzzz

Instructions:

1. In a medium bowl, add in the Greek yogurt, sour cream and Dijon mustard. Add in the chopped red onion, chopped mint, fresh lemon juice and hot sauce. Season with a dash of salt and black pepper. Whisk well until smooth in consistency.

2. Rinse the ground bulgur with warm water. Drain and place into a bowl. Set aside.

3. Place a large pot over medium heat. Add in 4 cups of water. Bring the water to a boil. Pour the water over the ground bulgur. Cover and set aside for 45 minutes to 1 hour.

4. In a large bowl, add in the ground beef. Add in the bulgur, chopped onion, chopped scallions, minced garlic, dried oregano, chopped mint leaves, extra virgin olive oil, dash of cayenne pepper and hot sauce. Season with a dash of salt and black pepper. Stir well until evenly blended.

5. Divide the dough into egg sized balls and form into an oval.

6. Place a large pot over medium heat. Pour in the canola oil and heat the oil until it reaches 350 degrees.

7. Add the kibbes into the oil. Fry for 5 minutes or until deep golden brown. Remove and place onto a large plate lined with paper towels to drain. Repeat with the remaining kibbes.

23) Brazilian Rabanada

This is the perfect traditional recipe that you can make during the Christmas holidays. For the tastiest results, be sure to serve this dish with a cup of fresh coffee.

Yield: 24 servings

Preparation Time: 50 minutes

Ingredient List:

- 24 slices of French baguette, sliced into thick slices
- 2 cups of whole milk
- 1 tablespoon of pure vanilla
- ½ to ¾ cup of white sugar
- 4 eggs, large and beaten
- Vegetable oil, for frying
- ½ cup of white sugar
- 1 tablespoon of ground cinnamon
- Maple syrup, for serving and optional

zzzzzzzzzzzzzzzzzzzzzzzzzzzzzzzzzzzzzzzzzzzzzzzzz

Instructions:

1. Line a large baking sheet with a few sheets of paper towels and set aside.

2. Divide the bread slices between two large baking dishes.

3. In a large bowl, add in the whole milk, pure vanilla and white sugar. Stir well to mix and pour over the bread slices. Set aside to soak for 20 minutes.

4. Place a large skillet over medium to high heat. Add in two inches of vegetable oil.

5. Dip the soaked bread slices in the beaten eggs on both sides. Place into the hot oil and cook for 1 to 1 ½ hours on both sides or until golden brown. Transfer to the baking sheets. Repeat with the remaining bread slices.

6. In a medium bowl, add in the white sugar and ground cinnamon. Stir well to mix.

7. Dredge the cooked bread slices into the cinnamon and sugar mixture.

8. Serve immediately with the maple syrup if you desire.

24) Brazilian Sopa de Fuba

This is another hearty soup dish that I know you won't be able to get enough of. Serve this with freshly baked bread for the perfect light lunch.

Yield: 6 servings

Preparation Time: 1 hour and 10 minutes

Ingredient List:

- ½ cup of yellow cornmeal
- 6 ounces of kielbasa sausage, cut into thin slices
- 7 cups of chicken stock
- 2 Tablespoons of canola oil
- 4 ounces of collard greens, sliced thinly and stemmed
- 2 eggs, beaten lightly
- Dash of salt and black pepper
- 2 scallions, thinly sliced

zzzzzzzzzzzzzzzzzzzzzzzzzzzzzzzzzzzzzzzzzzzzzzzz

Instructions:

1. Place a large skillet over the medium to high heat. Add in the cornmeal and cook for 3 to 4 minutes or until lightly toasted. Transfer to a small bowl and set aside.

2. Add the canola oil into the skillet. Once hot, add in the kielbasa sausages. Cook for 8 to 10 minutes or until browned. Remove and transfer to a large plate. Set aside.

3. Place a large stock pot over the high heat. Pour in the chicken stock and bring to a boil.

4. Add in the cornmeal and reduce the heat to low. Cook for 40 minutes or until the cornmeal is soft.

5. Add in the sausage and collards. Cook for 15 minutes or until the collard greens wilt.

6. In a medium bowl, add in the eggs and one cup of the cornmeal mixture. Whisk until smooth in consistency. Pour into the stockpot and stir well to incorporate.

7. Cook for an additional minute. Season with a dash of salt and black pepper.

8. Remove from heat and serve immediately. Garnish with the sliced scallions.

25) Brazilian Chocolate Fudge Flan

Unlike many traditional flan dishes that you can make, this flan is packed full of decadent chocolate taste that everyone with a sweet tooth will fall in love with.

Yield: 12 servings

Preparation Time: 4 hours and 45 minutes

Ingredients for the flan:

- 1, 14 ounce can of sweetened and condensed milk
- 14 ounces of whole milk
- 1 cup of unsweetened powdered cocoa
- 1/3 cup of white sugar
- 1 tablespoon + 1 teaspoon of all-purpose flour
- 1 tablespoon of unsalted butter, melted
- 4 eggs, large
- 1 tablespoon of pure vanilla
- Dash of salt
- Unsalted butter, for greasing
- Chocolate chips, for decoration and optional

Ingredients for the vanilla sauce:

- ½ cup of heavy whipping cream
- 1 pod of vanilla
- 1 tablespoon of white sugar

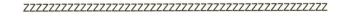

Instructions:

1. Preheat the oven to 350 degrees. Grease a large ring pan with butter.

2. In a large bowl, add in the condensed milk, whole milk, powdered cocoa, white sugar, all-purpose flour, butter, large eggs, pure vanilla and dash of salt. Stir well to mix and pour the mixture into the large ring pan.

3. Place into the oven to bake for 40 minutes. Remove and transfer to a wire rack to cool completely. Remove the cake from the pan and transfer to the fridge to chill.

4. Slice the pod of vanilla in half. Scrape the inside out and place into a small saucepan placed over medium heat. Add in the heavy cream and white sugar. Stir to mix and bring this mixture to a simmer. Remove from heat.

5. Pour the vanilla sauce over the cake.

6. Cover and place back into the fridge to chill for 3 to 4 hours. Serve when required.

About the Author

A native of Albuquerque, New Mexico, Sophia Freeman found her calling in the culinary arts when she enrolled at the Sante Fe School of Cooking. Freeman decided to take a year after graduation and travel around Europe, sampling the cuisine from small bistros and family owned restaurants from Italy to Portugal. Her bubbly personality and inquisitive nature made her popular with the locals in the villages and when she finished her trip and came home, she had made friends for life in the places she had visited. She also came home with a deeper understanding of European cuisine.

Freeman went to work at one of Albuquerque's 5-star restaurants as a sous-chef and soon worked her way up to head chef. The restaurant began to feature Freeman's original dishes as specials on the menu and soon after, she began to write e-books with her recipes. Sophia's dishes mix local flavours with European inspiration making them irresistible to the diners in her restaurant and the online community.

Freeman's experience in Europe didn't just teach her new ways of cooking, but also unique methods of presentation. Using rich sauces, crisp vegetables and meat cooked to perfection, she creates a stunning display as well as a delectable dish. She has won many local awards for her cuisine and she continues to delight her diners with her culinary masterpieces.

Author's Afterthoughts

I want to convey my big thanks to all of my readers who have taken the time to read my book. Readers like you make my work so rewarding and I cherish each and every one of you.

Grateful cannot describe how I feel when I know that someone has chosen my work over all of the choices available online. I hope you enjoyed the book as much as I enjoyed writing it.

Feedback from my readers is how I grow and learn as a chef and an author. Please take the time to let me know your thoughts by leaving a review on Amazon so I and your fellow readers can learn from your experience.

My deepest thanks,

Sophia Freeman

https://sophia.subscribemenow.com/

Made in the USA
Coppell, TX
01 November 2021